I0145909

Tales of the Golden Monkeys

Compiled by Yong Yange

1 Plus Books
China Pictorial Press

Tales of the Golden Monkeys

©2017 China Pictorial Press
©2017 1 Plus Books   English Edition

ISBN-13: 978-0-9997514-0-4

English Translator: Zhong Yuanshan
Special Editor: Sophia Liu
Book Design: Ai Qing
Published by 1 Plus Publishing & Consulting in the USA
www.1plusbooks.com
San Francisco, USA

Preface

China faces a heavy task in promoting economic growth as a developing country. Nevertheless, with regard to global climate change and environmental protection, the Chinese government, in recent years, has been advancing a development concept of "innovation, coordination, green, open and sharing", taking green development and a low-carbon and circular economy to the next level. Unprecedented priority has been given to eco-environmental protection. Wild animals are the spirits of nature, and those endangered rare species are very sensitive factors in the eco-environment. With special habits and unique survival wisdom, they harmonize perfectly with the successive beauty of the different seasons and, along with China's diverse geographical environment and rich fauna and flora, constitute the natural environment without which we cannot exist.

China has a long history of thousands of years. It not only

has a profound cultural heritage, but also rich ecological diversity, and a wide variety of wild animals is one of the highlights. China has always been committed to the ecological/environmental cause and has made great progress in the wild animal protection. According to the 2011 National Wildlife Resource Survey, China's rare and endangered wildlife protection has achieved remarkable results: the survival status of a number of endangered wild animals such as the Golden Monkeys, Asian elephants, Père David's deer, giant pandas, crested ibis, Tibetan antelopes, etc., has improved and significant population increases. Among the 420 species listed in the *Lists of Widelife under Special State Protection*, the populations of 341, are no longer considered endangered. At the same time, however, the situation of wildlife protection in China is still very serious, 87.7% of the wild animals are face a squeeze on their living space due to habitat reduction, fragmentation, deterioration, human activity, etc.; many important habitats and bird cluster activity areas and migration channels are challenged by land development, agricultural reclamation, environmental pollution and other threats.

It is of great significance to protect wild animals, save rare and endangered wild animals and maintain biodiversity and ecological balance according to law, for promoting the harmonious development of humans and nature and enhancing the construction of a true ecological civilization. I hope that this colorful, dynamic life pictorial on Chinese wild animals will enable the general adult readers to embark on a unique trip through the natural beauty on Earth, while drawing their attention to the fate of China's rare wild animals and encouraging them to become actively involved in the protection movement along with us. We can build a new pattern of broad participation in wildlife protection and make due contributions to the construction of a beautiful China with a good ecological civilization and improvement of the global environment!

The Compiler
Nov.2017

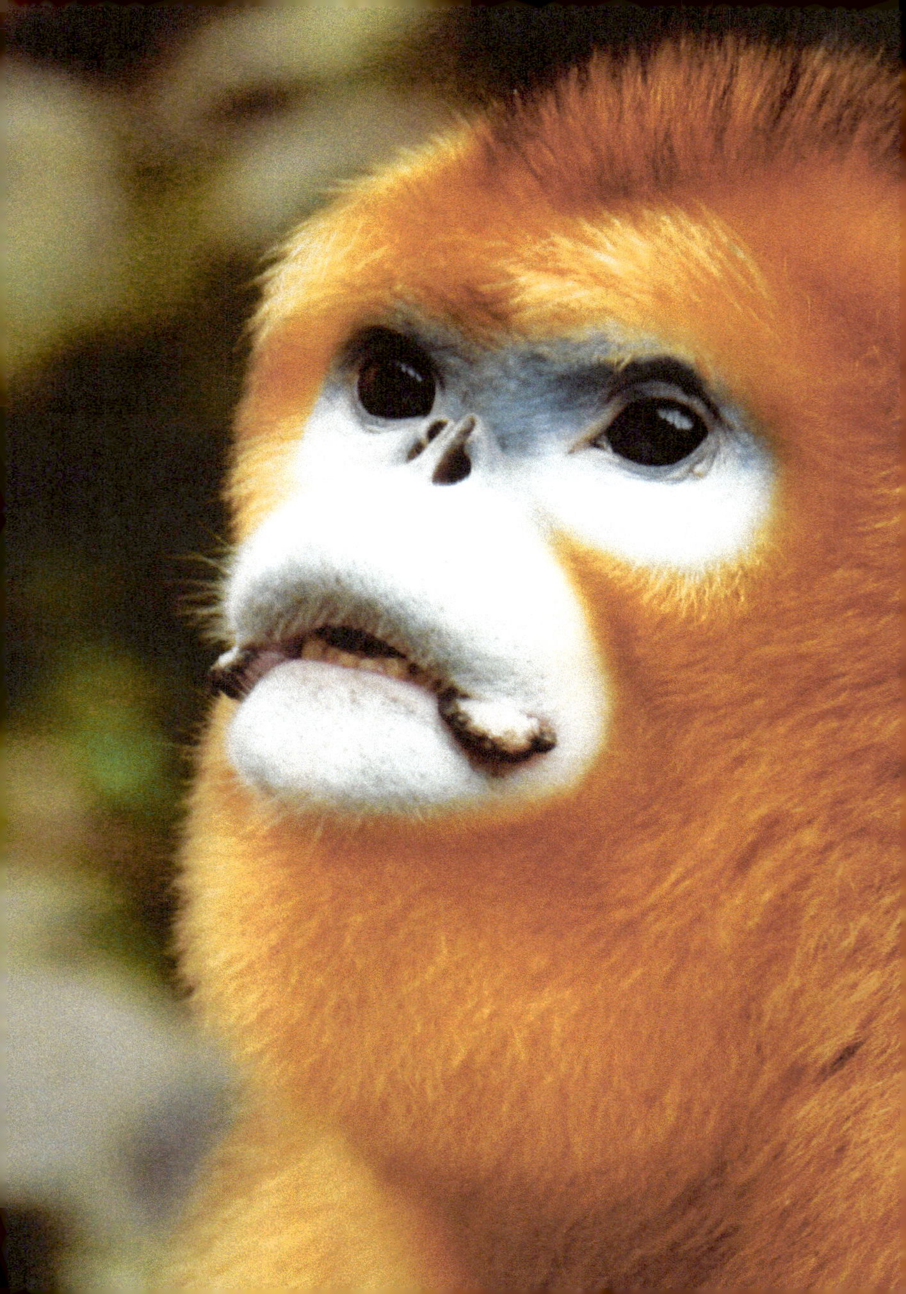

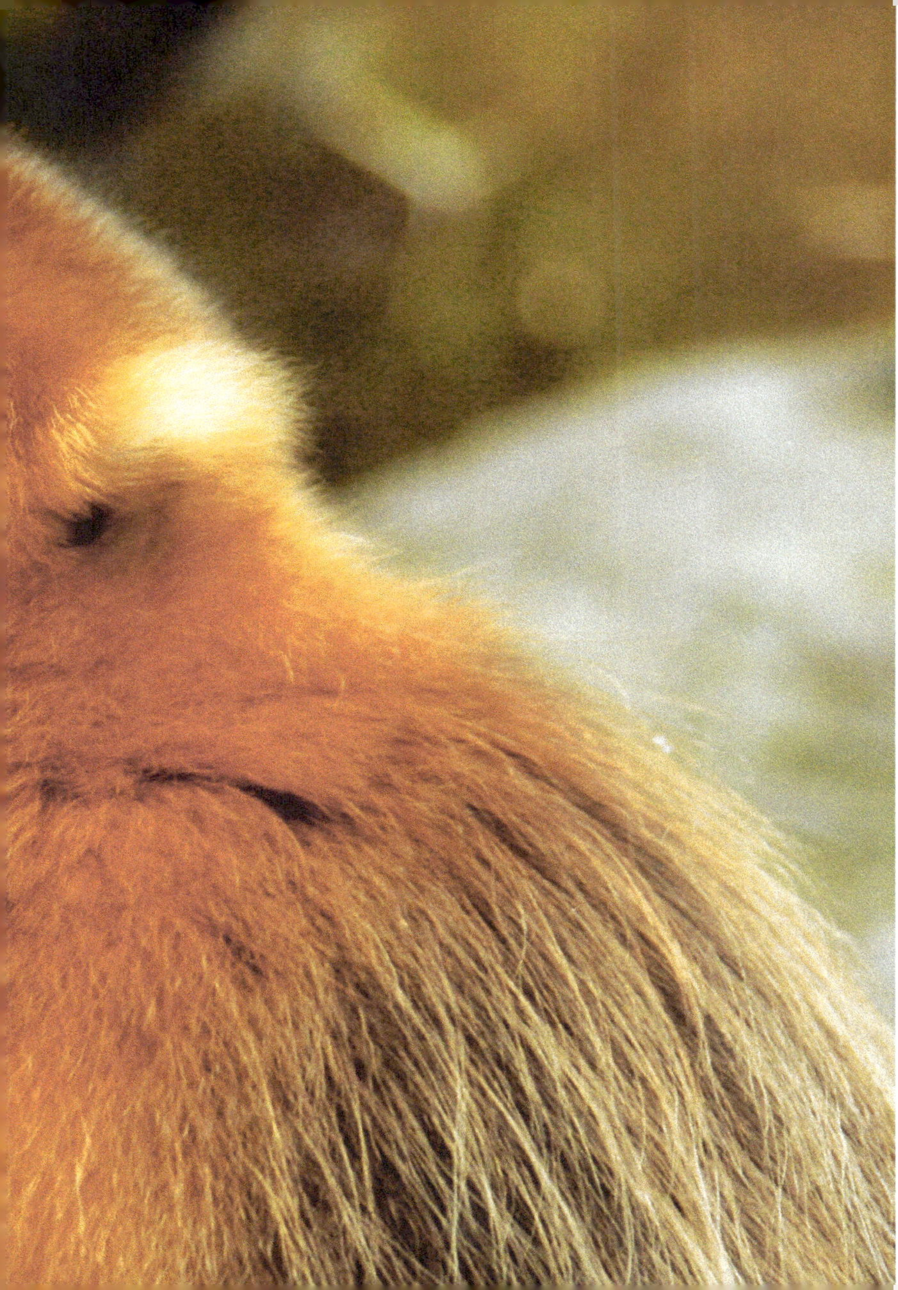

CONTENTS

I

Native
Chinese Monkeys

The Golden Monkeys, or Sichuan Snub-nosed Monkeys, with the scientific name of *Rhinopithecus roxelana*, is classified as a snub-nosed monkeys of Colobinae under Cercopithecidae of Primatesa (Old World Monkeys of the Colombinae Primate family). It has a cave-nose bridge and pitching-up nostrils. Its hair is golden and bright as silk, hence its usual names.

There are four kinds of such monkeys in the world, three of them in China. In addition to the Sichuan Snub-nosed Monkey (Rhinopithecus roxelana), there are Yunnan Golden Monkeys (Rhinopithecus bieti), Guizhou Golden Monkeys

(Rhinopithecus brelichi) and Vietnam Golden Monkeys (Rhinopithecus avunculus). However, their coat color is not "golden" and they are actually called "golden monkeys"for convenience of scientific classification.

The Sichuan Golden Monkeys are an unique species in China, distributed across western Sichuan, southern Shaanxi, western Hubei (Shennongjia), southern Gansu, and Chongqing (Wushan). They live in deep mountains and lead a group life. With a golden "cloak" on their back, they climb trees and can execute flying jumps from one to another.

The Golden Monkeys described in this book mainly refers to those living in the mountains of Shaanxi province's Qinling Range. They are concentrated at the northern and southern sides of the central massif. The habitat involves a narrow area from Taibai in the west to Zhashui in the east, covering about 2,000 square km, and vertically distributed in the coniferous and broad-leaved mixed forests and sub-alpine coniferous forests at an elevation from 1000 to 3000 meters. They live a typical arboreal life.

The total number of Golden Monkeys in Qinling Mountains is currently only 3,500 to 4,000. They have strange appearance and coat hair. An adult monkey weighs about 15 kg, with a body length of about 50 cm and a tail length of about 60 cm; the male is bigger than the female. Their eyes are dark brown, face blue, nostrils pitched up, lips short, thick and prominent and the mouth is round. A male adult golden monkey has a sarcoidosis-like tuber at its canine point, and this tuber grows larger with age and gradually becomes dark brown from the original meat red. It has a dark brown tufty forehead, while the hair is brown on its cheeks and forehead, light yellow-white on its chest and belly, and golden, long and bright as silk on its upper arms, shoulders and back (a male has longer hair than the female), creating an extraordinary style. It starts molting from April and ending in August every year, and its coat hair is the most brilliant in autumn and winter.

The Golden Monkeys have strong lower limbs and is very good at jumping. Even if two trees are far apart, they can shake a tree branch to provide leverage for the jump. Its tail is almost as long as the body and plays a balancing role, which is the result of their long-term adaptation to the arboreal life.

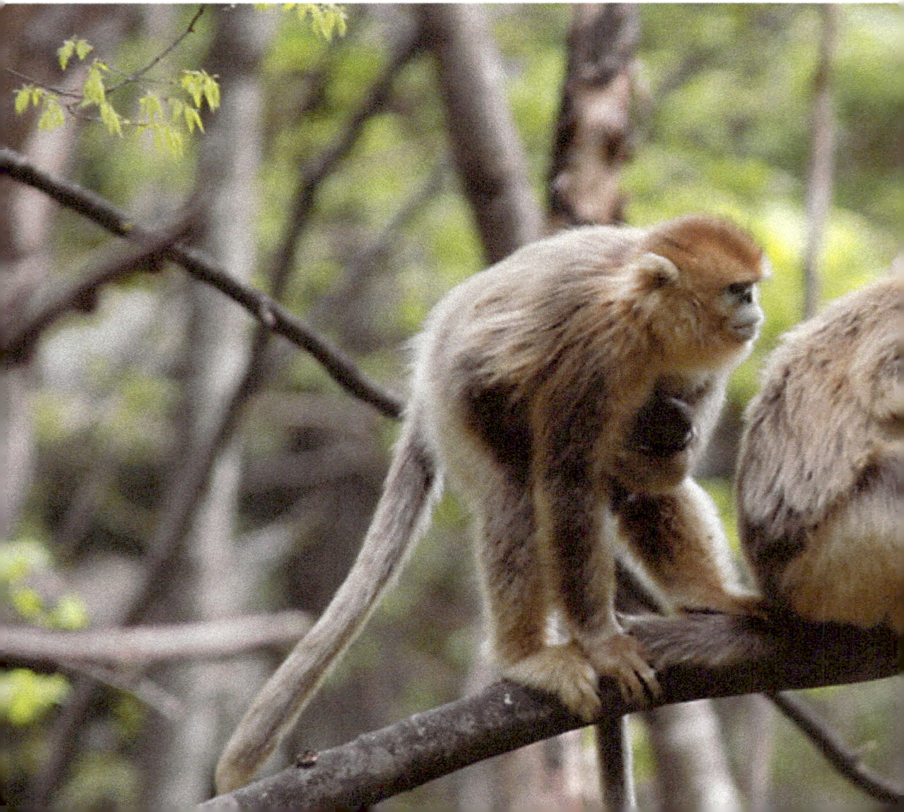

II

Association
Characteristics of
Golden Monkeys

The Golden Monkey lives a typically gregarious family life, and its population structure involves many small families forming a distinctive society. Each family society contains as few as 30 to 50 or as many as 300 monkeys, covering old, middle-aged, young and infant monkeys. Regardless of size, each group has a number of small families, and each family has 1 to 2 (depending on the size of the group) strong males acting as "sentinels".

Sentinel monkeys, also known as "guard monkeys", take on the duty of protecting the safety of the entire group. During family activity or while resting, they are scattered on the alert in the surrounding heights, and will immediately call out "hoo-ha, hoo-ha" at the sight of any enemy closing in. Then, all the monkeys will quickly flee.

Every family has its own dominant parent. These maintain the unity of the small families and take on the burden of protecting their interests. Family groups are well organized in collective action; little monkeys and mothers

carrying babies stay in the middle of the team, and strong male monkeys guard the front and rear. Monkey groups have good physical agility; they can disappear instantly without trace at the first hint of an abnormal situation. Once the danger passes, they can be heard playing with joyful noises one after another. Therefore, in the jungles, people often hear monkey sounds but hardly ever catch a glimpse of them.

It is a common impression that every monkey group has a majestic "monkey king". In fact, the monkey community has parents rather than kings.

In monkey society, a family is a unit and under the leadership of the parent (big male monkey).

For population optimization, this male serving as the parent is often more robust than other monkeys, and has a larger body, more golden and shiny hair, and a more charming pale blue face. The parent in the family must first have strong breeding and mating ability. A male monkey in sexual maturity can gradually replace the original parent if he can take over more females. A parent will abdicate and be replaced by a new one with advancing age and declining reproductive ability.

A parent is always in the forefront of the family. At rest, it will find the most favorable position to sit down, and take responsibility for group protection. It will sometimes glance at other groups, and open its mouth to show sharp teeth at other times. Behind it will be a group of female monkeys carrying children.

Families can contain a different numbers of monkeys in the same family group. Sometimes, a large male (parent) has a dozen attached female and their children, perhaps numbering more than 20 individuals. In most families, however, the total number of females and children possessed by a big male is only seven or eight.

Internal disputes are inevitable in large families. For family stability and unity, the big male often jumps up and down, and pacifies his wives by means of mounting, scratching, and grooming. He is more generous to his children, hugging them, and fully shows his honorable status as the parent.

Inside a family, members abide by certain

orders when eating. Pregnant females are given priority, followed by the big male, other females and their children.

The Golden Monkeys have strong maternal instincts. Scientists engaged in a field study once saw a sorrowful female monkey carrying the body of her dead baby for more than a month, not wishing to put it away even when running and migrating with the group.

A baby monkey will get love from most family members. The mother will let other females carry the baby, just like aunts and sisters in the human world. Some little disputes inevitably occur when they fight to hold the baby at times.

A baby monkey tightly grasps the mother's body hair, hoping to find the opportunity to suck on the teats, and from time to time moving its small head away from the mother's chest and looks around with bright eyes. The baby monkeys are pale yellow, with metallic luster. When staying together, they look like tender yellow woolen balls jostling about.

The semi-adult golden monkeys are some who are the loveliest "stars of the show". Their coat color is beige, darker than their younger brothers and sisters and lighter than their parents who are golden. They can no longer rely on their mothers, and play within their own habitat according to their own preferences. They sometimes catch hold of a companion's tail as a toy, hold a soft branch and jump between trees, show off their stunts with vines on a cliff, and yet come together in a blue funk getting ready to follow their parents to escape. Once the danger passes, they will immediately put on a new "show". Some little male monkeys learn to serve as "sentinels", and some little females will take on the active care of their younger siblings for their mothers and aunts.

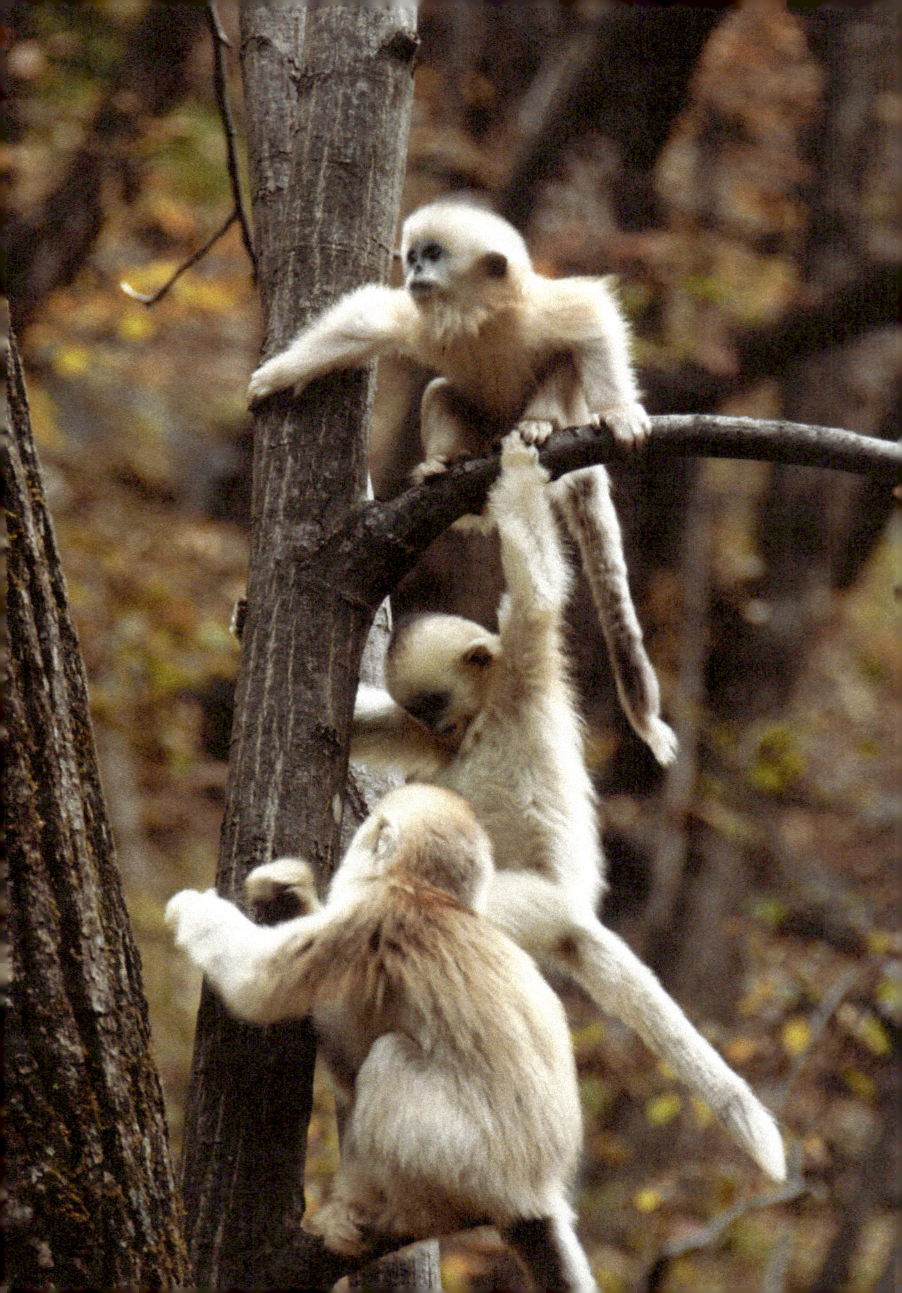

Fights can often be seen between families. The aggressive attacks are mostly intimidation rather than involving severe tearing, and often end with one side avoiding the other thereafter.

Within a group, a family with more members holds higher status. When foraging, the biggest family often takes the lead to enter a rich area and enjoy a meal, followed by lower families picking up the residual food. Bachelor monkeys are the last to eat the dregs left by others. As the name suggests, bachelor monkeys are groups of male monkeys living outside of the families often threatened and attacked by the dominant male.

Monkeys in a family group live a collective life, but contacts are rarely seen between other families. "Parentage"is not a life-long system, and those bachelors unwilling to accept their inferior status will challenge the monkey ruler. They are ready to take advantage of any weak point to steal one or more wives of a "parent", going off to a distant place to be promoted to the rank of "parent", and blend into other monkey groups. Some "bachelor monkeys" can wait for such a chance with good results; others cannot take away a wife from the current "parents" and remain as lifelong bachelors often threatened by attack from the whole group. Those brave "bachelor monkeys" with a challenging spirit will always pay a close attention to the "parents", and take immediate action to replace them once the big male becomes weak.

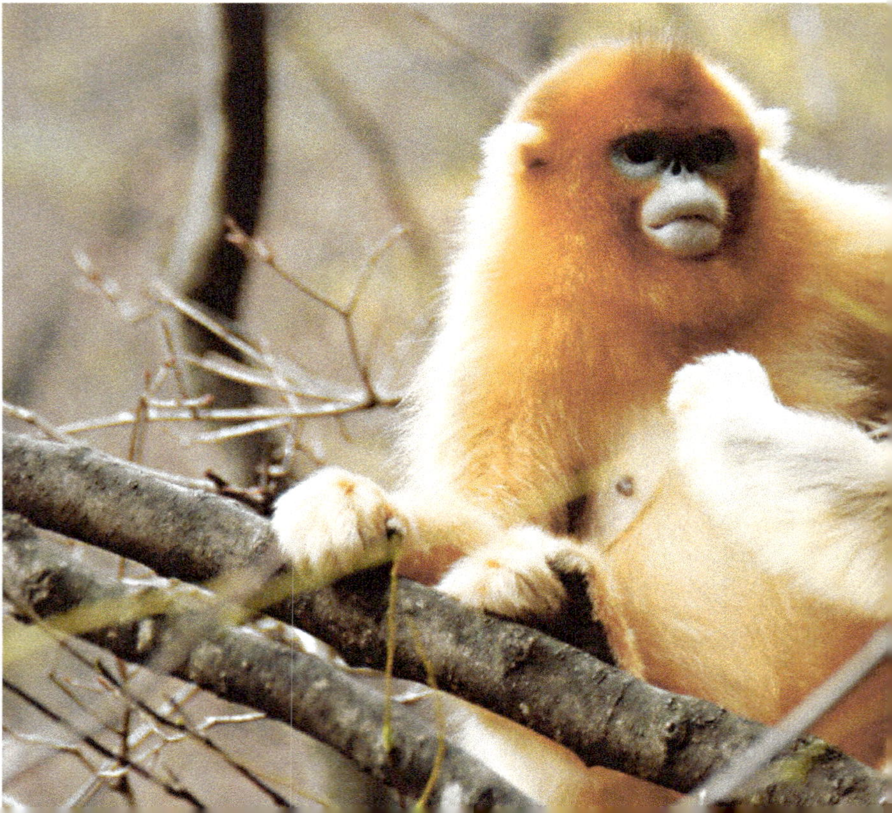

🐒 III
Individual Behavior of Golden Monkeys

The various acts of animals have been formed in the process of evolution in order to adapt to the living environment. Through long-term observation and study, scientists confirmed Sichuan Golden Monkey has 54 kinds of typical behavior and action modes. These are divided into non-social behavior (individual solitary behavior) and social behavior (inter-individual communication behavior).

Non-social behavior includes: sleeping, sitting, walking and running alone, self-care grooming, drinking water, finding food, and eating alone.

Social behavior covers seven types: intimate, domineering, threatening, aggressive, yielding, reproductive, maternity and child behavior, and each has several specific acts.

☐ Intimate behavior

• Approach: An individual monkey walks up to another, getting ever closer.

• Leave: An individual approaches another monkey, and the latter stands up and leaves; or two individuals stay together, and one of them leaves.

• Follow: An individual monkey walks around followed by another.

- Sitting together: Two individuals sit together, contacting each other with the body, but their arms and legs do not intersect or embrace.

- Quick grooming: This act means comfort and reconciliation and occurs on invitation, especially after a conflict between two parties. One monkey provides a quick, brief grooming to show comfort or reconciliation.

- Grooming: An individual cleans the fur and hair of another. The grooming monkey takes a sitting position, teases the hair of the groomed one, opens its mouth slightly, issues a slight click and from time to time touches the hair with its mouth to clean up foreign matter.

• Kissing the back: When holding waist, the sponsor will also press with its mouth or lick the recipient's waist.

• Holding the waist: This act means amity, or, sometimes, a slight punishment. An individual holds another monkey's waist from behind and sometimes also pulls the other towards its embrace. Often the initiatoris superior to the recipient.

• Hug: Two individuals get belly-to-belly. One or both stretch out the arms to cling together; one puts its head on the other's chest or shoulder, and their tails surround their bodies. Their faces look relaxed and sometimes they issue a soft crooning noise.

• Touch: An individual touches another monkey's body.

• Shake hands: An individual pulls at another monkey's hand.

• Catch or take: An individual monkey catches or takes another's food; the latter may allow this or seek to grab the food back, threatening the grabber, or even fighting.

• Open mouth: One monkey will open its mouth, but not show its teeth clearly.

• Playing games: This behavior often occurs among infantile and juvenile monkeys. Two individuals open the mouth halfway, relaxing their facial muscles, and shake their heads slightly. There are diverse games, such as catching or patting the other's head or shoulder, advancing or withdrawing head to head, twisting together to roll, chasing each other, catching up and running.

• Begging for food: An individual extends its mouth to another monkey who is eating, asking for food. Most initiators are young monkeys.

• Eye communication: An individual looks into the eyes of another monkey, and guides the latter to pay attention to or watch a situation or object.

☐ Domineering behavior

- Domineering: This behavior is done to show the individual's social status and strong physical behavior in the group. The animal makes forceful moves and makes a loud noise and shows its power and prestige by such acts as jouncing, rushing, and shaking trees. This act often occurs at the time of group migration.
- Substitute: An individual with superior social status takes over the advantageous place (such as cool or warm location, or some convenient place for food) from one with inferior social status. This action is called "taking the place", while the other side's ceding of the territory is called "avoidance behavior".

☐ Threatening behavior

• Staring: This behavior indicates a possible threat. The initiator bends its head forward, closes its mouth and stares at the other monkey.

• Staring and clucking: The initiator leans its head forward, closes its mouth, stares, and also clucks to issue a cuckoo-like call.

• Staring each other: This is two-way threatening behavior; the two sides of the conflict stand face to face and stare at each other intently.

• Parade step: An individual bends forward with its head, closes its mouth, and walks in parade steps directly towards another monkey. This behavior means denouncing someone publicly for its crime.

☐ Aggressive behavior

• Catch or hit: An individual monkey catches or hits another.

• Rush: An individual rushes at another monkey and stops; the other side will stand still to resist or will escape.

- Wrestle: In the event of conflict, both sides stretch out the hands to catch each other's hair on the head, neck, shoulder and other parts. Sometimes one monkey can seize the other's hair, lift it up and throw it down.

• Catch up: An individual monkey catches up with another; the latter runs in the front and the former chases it over a long distance.

• Biting: An individual bites another monkey's body.
This behavior is the most aggressive one.

☐ Yielding behavior

• Curling up: This is when a monkey adopts a sitting posture, bends forward its upper body, shrugs and bows with eyebrows relaxed, eyes down, sometimes mouth open, chin adducted, forearms on the thighs, hands on the knees, legs curled up and closed together under the body, and the tail naturally drooping.

- Retreat: When an individual is threatened, or attacked, it will face the opponent, take a few steps backward or take a few steps away, and then resume the confrontation.

Tales of the Golden Monkeys

• Escape: When an individual is threatened, or attacked, and seeks to escape.

Reproductive behavior

• Creeping: Before sexual behavior, a female will issue an invitation to a male by means of creeping, which is regarded as sexual invitation behavior. The female will look at the male at first, casting amorous glances and then running for a little while. Then it presses its face and belly close to the ground, bends its front legs, brings its rear legs close to the belly, lowers its tail, and gets ready to accept male mating.Other primates also have such sexual invitation behavior, but they mostly shake their hips or heads. Only the Golden Monkeys adopt creeping as the invitation.

• Mounting: Sexual behavior begins with the male mounting the female. The male bends forward, presses its belly against the female's back, catches hold of the back, with head down and tail naturally drooping, and sometimes issuing soft noises. At the same time, the female raises her rear and sometimes turns her head to look gently at the male. Penile insertion then takes place followed by ejaculation.

• Curl up: In view of the function, this behavior corresponds to "showing hip" behavior of other primates. The Golden Monkey curls up, instead of showing its hip, to yield when threatened.

• Open mouth: This act is common in Sichua Golden Monkeys' social interaction and is a important mode of reconciliation behavio Adult males, especially parents, open the mouths while walking to express amity an harmlessness, similar to the open-hande waving of human beings. This is complete different from other animals that mostly ope their mouths to indicate a threat or attack.

The following behaviors are typical, unique and distinct from other primates.

• Stare and cluck: This act is an important and common threatening behavior of Sichuan Golden Monkeys. An individual stares at another monkey, closes its mouth, and issues a cuckoo-like sound. The longer the sound, the stronger the threat. It is completely different from other animals which open their mouths to shout and threaten others.

• Retreat: When an individual is threatened, or attacked, although in a weak position, it will not escape immediately, but will face the opponent, take a few steps backward or to the side, and then confront each other. This act means unwillingness to yield and can be seen only in societies where the hierarchical relationship is not very strict.

• Parade step: An individual monkey (mostly adult males) approaches another with closed mouth and parade steps to show a threatening posture. When opening the mouth, Golden Monkeys show amity, and when closing it, they are being threatening.

• Quick grooming: In the event of a struggle, there is a series of reconciliation acts, such as opening the mouth, hugging, sitting, shaking hands and grooming; quick grooming is the most common behavior. Except for reconciliation, this act can be seen in the invitation of grooming, and one side will finish quickly to soothe the other side.

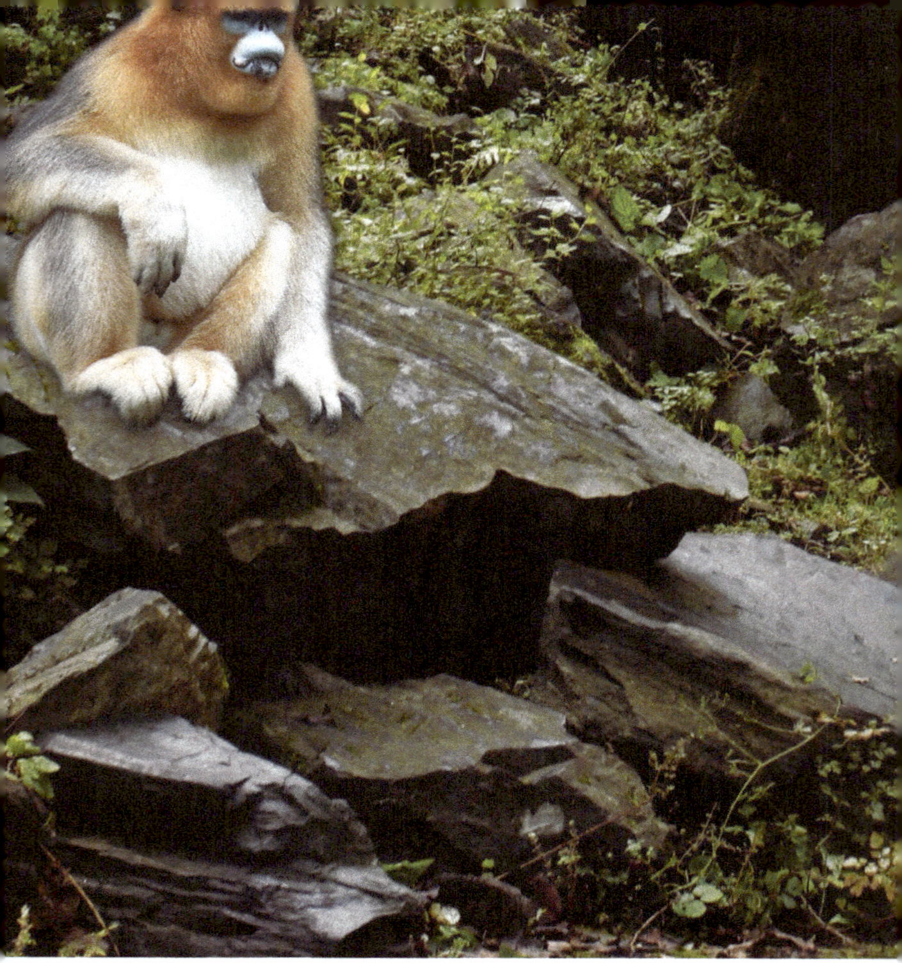

Individual Behavior of Golden Monkeys

• Staring at each other: This is two-way threatening behavior or a response to the threat of another. It is closely related to the relatively loose social hierarchy of the Golden Monkeys. Confrontational behavior cannot be seen in other animal groups where the hierarchical relationship is very strict.

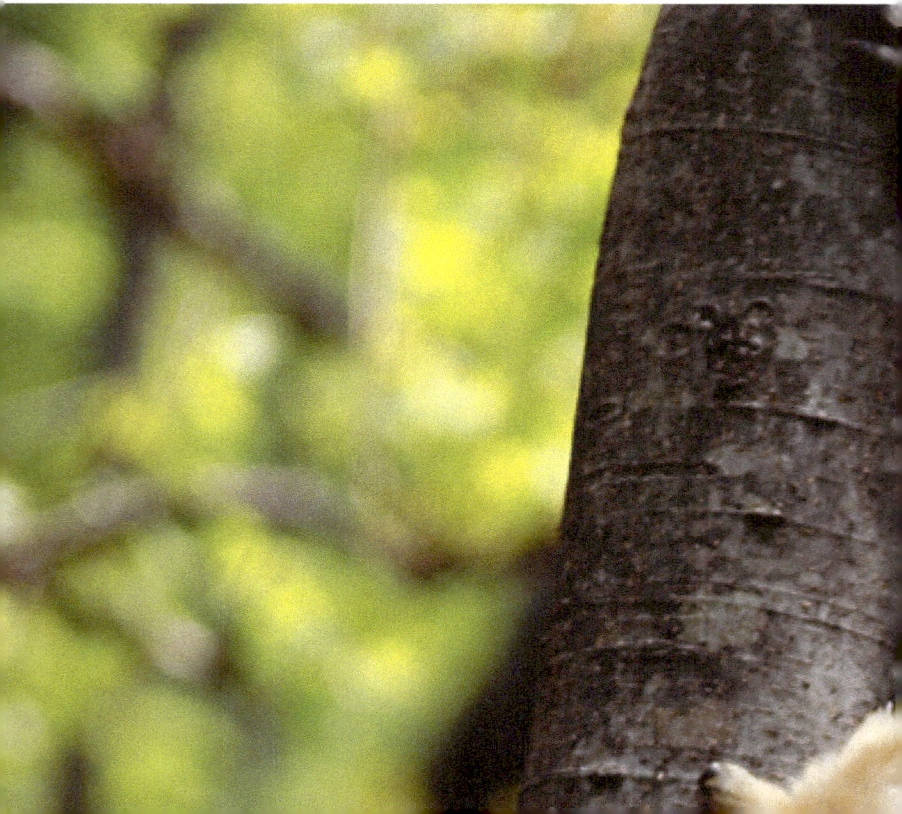

IV
Routine of Golden Monkeys

The Golden Monkeys follow a regular daily routine. Daytime activities include feeding, resting, grooming, moving round, and so on. Wild Golden Monkeys have two feeding peaks during the daytime activities, respectively in the morning and afternoon. They have a long break at noon. Feeding and resting are their main activities, accounting for 62% of the total. There are significant differences between seasons. Usually resting accounts for a higher percentage in summer and autumn than in spring and winter. At sunrise, the Golden Monkeys begin their feeding activities. After a few hours of moving and feeding, the monkeys stop to rest in the

tall trees on mountain ridges from 11 to 12 in the morning. During this time, the monkeys do not move, and each family occupies one to two trees. It is the best time to identify family groups, families, and individual relationships. The monkeys start to feed again at 2 to 3 p.m., and at sunset they rest in groups in the coniferous trees over. Usually the young monkeys are in the center surrounded by adult monkeys both for protection from predators and shelter from cold and wind. From May to August every year, the groups migrate to higher mountains to escape the summer heat. After August or September, they

migrate back to the lower mountains to harvest the fruits of autumn.

At rest, some Golden Monkeys lie down on the trunk to sleep, while those not sleeping groom each other. When grooming, they occasionally catch some kind of small thing to eat that was once thought to be lice. In reality, a monkey's skin secretes some salt-like crystals forming an indispensable nutrient for monkeys. They find and eat these salt crystals embedded in each other's hair, which not only represents mutual intimacy but also has importance for obtaining

nutrients.

When winter comes, and the last leaves fall, the northern snow arrives on schedule. Bark and buds are major winter foods for the Golden Monkeys. Living in the cold Qinling mountains, their stomach has become tougher. However, bark and buds alone cannot provide them with enough energy, and the monkeys need to snuggle together to maintain body temperature. In winter, the Golden Monkeys can live at places with an elevation as low as 800 meters.

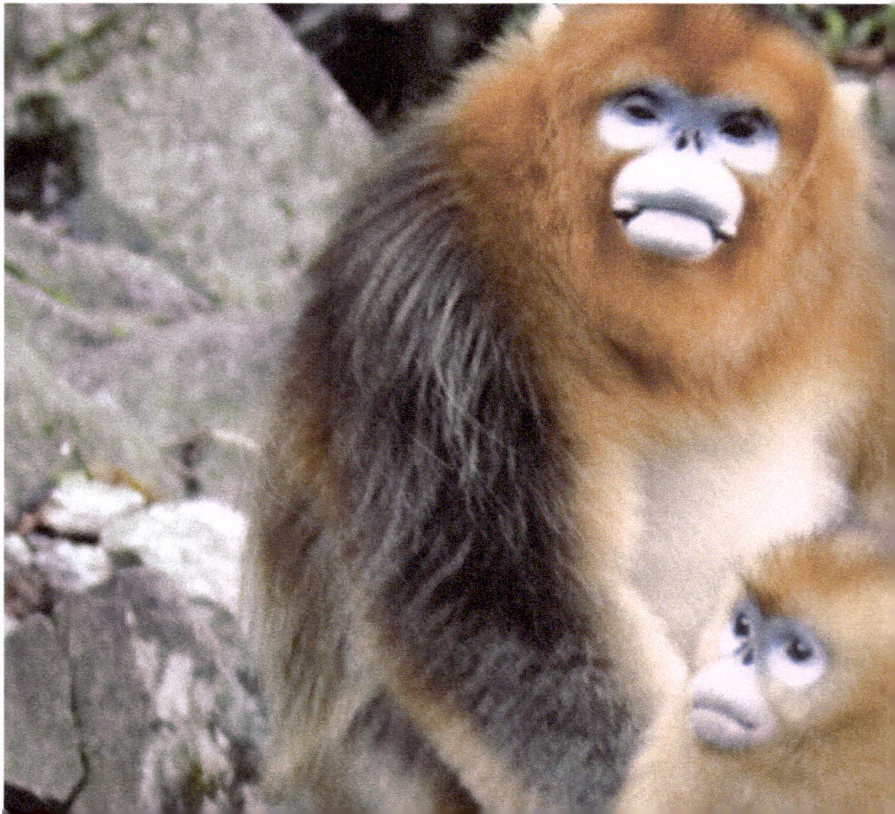

V
Reproductive Characteristics of Golden Monkeys

The Golden Monkeys start to engage in sexual behavior at an age of three to four, but only achieve sexual maturity and a reproductive capacity at age five or six. The major annual mating period is from September to November, and the mating activities are relatively concentrated during this time. A male golden monkey can mate with two or three females each day. In the mating period, female monkeys have relatively strong sexual desire due to ovulation, and often take the initiative in courtship. During the courtship display, a female goes in front of a male, stretches its two forelimbs, crouches down on the ground or on a horizontal trunk, and

raises its hip (that is, creeping). The male reacts
by beginning to mount for mating. The mating
action often lasts for 10 to 20 seconds.

The pregnancy lasts about seven months, the
birth occurring largely in March or April. A
mother gives birth to one baby every two years.
If a baby dies in an accident, however, the mother
will give birth again in the following year. Single
births are the norm, and twins are very rare.

Newborn Golden Monkeys have gray brown hair that will gradually become milky yellow after 15 days and gray after one year. Mothers show strong care, always keeping their offspring tightly in their arms, or let the babies get hold of their armpits or bellies while walking, and lift babies' tails from time to time to smell whether there has been defecation. When a baby monkey reaches one, the mother begins to wean it, although the little monkey starts to live independently only at the age of four or five years old.

• Newborn baby monkey.

• Child monkey.

• Sub-adult monkey.

• Young male monkey.

• Young female monkey.

- Adult male monkey.

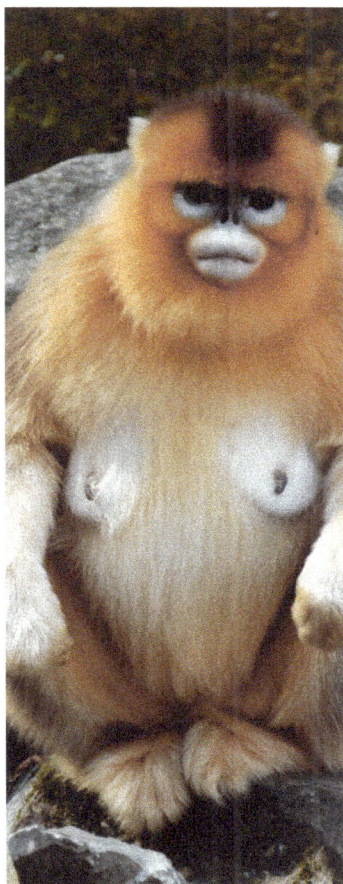

- Adult female monkey.

VI
Living Environment
of Golden Monkeys

The Golden Monkeys in the Qinling Mountain Range are distributed at elevations from 1,200 to 2,400 meters. At the upper limit for living are dark coniferous forests with a single tree species, so there is less food resources available. The 1200-meter lower limit living can be breached in theory, but then the monkeys tend to come into contact with humans beings, and human production and living interferences with monkey activities thus forcing them to go higher.

The main habitats of Qinling Golden Monkeys span two vertical vegetation belts.In low mountains and medium mountains with an elevation from 800 to 1800 meters lies a warm

temperate deciduous broad-leaved forest belt. Deciduous broad-leaved trees mainly include cork oaks, quercus, and Quercus acutissima, followed by Platycarya, lacquer trees, chestnut trees,Castanea seguinii dobe shell oaks, and so on. The coniferous trees are mainly composed of Pinus tabulaeformis and Pinus armandii, and in the lower area there are Pinus massoniana. There are also evergreen broadleaf trees in the area, but the amount is significantly reduced. There are Bashania fargesii in the forest belt with an elevation above 1,800 meters, and the animals living there include giant panda, golden monkey, large and small civet, golden cat, leopard, porcupine, musk deer, dog badger, roe deer, and so on.

In the mountains with elevations from 1,800 to 2,400 meters stands a coniferous and broad-leaved mixed forest belt. In the area at an elevation below 2,300 meters is the Huashan pine, hemlock and broadleaf mixed forest sub-zone. The dominant species of coniferous

forest are Pinus armandii and hemlock, and pines (lower), spruces or Bashan firs are rarely seen there. The major broad-leaved species include red and white birch, as well as Populus davidiana, lacquer trees, Carpinus, etc.; the dominant species is Pinus armandii. In the area above 2300 meters is the red birch and fir mixed forest sub-zone. The amount of firs and spruces increases significantly, and there is a small amount of hemlock and Pinus armandii. Broad-leaved species include red birch and Betula utilis, and the associated species there include white birch, bright birch, Betula chinensis, Carpinus polyneura, and Populus davidiana. The dominant species in the sub-zone are red birch and Betula utilis, and in some places, there are birch forests. Animals in this area include golden monkey, small civet, golden cat, muntjac, hairy deer, porcupine, wolf, musk deer and blood pheasant.

Companion plants

• Red Autumnal Leaves.

• Codonopsis Pilosula.

☐ Companion animals

• Squirrel.

• Musk Deer.

• Hyak.

• Giant Panda.

• Hog Badger.

In the mountains with elevations from 1,800 to 2,400 meters stands a coniferous and broad-leaved mixed forest belt. In the area at an elevation below 2,300 meters is the Huashan pine, hemlock and broadleaf mixed forest sub-zone. The dominant species of coniferous forest are Pinus armandii and hemlock, and pines (lower), spruces or Bashan firs are rarely seen there. The major broad-leaved species include red and white birch, as well as Populus davidiana, lacquer trees, Carpinus, etc.; the dominant species is Pinus armandii. In the area above 2300 meters is the red birch and fir mixed forest sub-zone. The amount of firs and spruces increases significantly, and there is a small amount of hemlock and Pinus armandii. Broad-leaved species include red birch and Betula utilis, and the associated species there include white birch, bright birch, Betula chinensis, Carpinus polyneura, and Populus davidiana. The dominant species in the sub-zone are red birch and Betula utilis, and in some places, there are birch forests. Animals in this area include golden monkey, small civet, golden cat, muntjac, hairy deer, porcupine, wolf, musk deer and blood pheasant.

• Spring Habitat.

• Summer Habitat.

• Autumn Habitat.

• Winter Habitat.

☙ VII
Feeding Habits of Golden Monkeys

The Sichuan Golden Monkey is an omnivorous animal, but its staple food is plants, such as young leaves of trees, epiphytic filamentous lichens attached to trees, Chinese Usnea, and epiphytic filamentous lichens attached to big tree bark. They eat a variety of buds, fresh leaves, flowers, tender roots, and rattans, bamboo shoots, and wild fungi in spring and summer, and eat a variety of leaves, seeds, berries, nuts, and barks in autumn and winter. There are more than 30 kinds of plants within them, the common ones being ligustrun lucidum, ligustrum quihoui, Chinese birch, Salix caprea, Salix sinopurpurea, Ulmus parvifolia, Euonymus japonicus, Buxus sinica, Chinese Usnea, etc. They occasionally eat insects and bird eggs.

• Hazel nut.

• Hericium Erinaceus.

• Kiwi fruit.

VIII
Survival Strategies of
Golden Monkeys

☐ Common Diseases

Golden Monkeys can live up to 17 years in captivity, but the usual lifespan is 15 years. The lifespan of those in the wild is not yet determined as the monkeys are prone to many diseases.

Digestive system diseases: For those Golden Monkeys fed artificially, the common disease is dyspepsia, with symptoms of a bloated stomach, hiccups, as well as intestinal obstruction due to intussusception.

Internal parasites: The common internal parasites include hairy nematode (also known as whipworm), followed by roundworm. They are mainly parasitic, living in the digestive tract, and a large number of parasites can cause

gastrointestinal complications.

Age-related diseases: Such diseases mainly involve oral problems, including gingival hyperplasia, root inflammation, gum erosion, tooth loss and alveolar inflammation, and may lead to decay and death of eating difficulties and nutritional deficiency.

☐ Grouping Phenomenon

In winter and spring, the seasons most lacking in food resources, the population of a single Golden Monkey group is 20 to 50 in most cases, while the largest group never exceeds 100. However, in summer and autumn, the seasons rich in food resources, you can see large monkey

groups with populations of 100 to 200 and even more. The obvious cause for the winter and spring grouping habits is food shortage, as it is easier for a small group to find sufficient food. In summer and autumn, however, it is beneficial to live in large groups for reproduction and social exchange.

The hair color of the Sichuan Golden Monkey varies with the seasons.Every spring, they begin to take off their long hair and adopt short hair to keep cool and adapt to the summer heat. In spring and summer, dark gray is the major color of their hair. As the leaves turn yellow or red in autumn, their hair becomes long again and changes to golden yellow or yellow-red color. The change of the hair color is consistent with the hue of the broadleaf forests, which plays a role of protective coloration and is the result of adaptation to many generations of arboreal life.

• Spring hair color.

• Spring and summer hair color.

• Autumn and winter hair color.

IX
Companion Animals of Golden Monkeys

The Sichuan Golden Monkey distributed in the Qinling Mountains has similar companion animals to those distributed in Sichuan, Hubei and Gansu. Many of the companion animals fall into the first-ranked protection category, such as giant panda, leopard, takin, forest musk deer, etc. Those falling into the second category include jackal, black bear, yellow throat mink, otter, big civet, small civet, gold cat, gazelle, goral, etc. In addition, the wild boar, porcupine, burnt deer and bamboo rat live here. Rare birds include the blood pheasant, red-belly tragopan, spoon chicken, red-belly pheasant, etc., as well as rusty-cheeked scimitar-babbler, streak-breasted scimitar babbler, Elliot's laughingthrush, white-throated laughingthrush, Aethopyga gouldiae, Red-billed Leiothrix, etc. There are also many mountain reptiles and amphibians.

In the wild environment, the natural enemies of Golden Monkeys are mainly large raptors, and juvenile monkeys are the most vulnerable.

Golden bush robin

Giant panda

Red-billed Leiothrix

Elliot's Laughingthrush

Golden eagle

Aethopyga

Takin

Muntiacus reevesi

Golden pheasant

Ring-necked pheasant

🐒 X
Ecological Worries:
Threats from Humans

Compared with natural enemies, humans are a bigger threat to the Golden Monkeys. The skin is expensive and is used as high-level fur raw material. Furthermore, this has the function of cold and moisture protection, and it is thought to be able to drive out evil spirits. Its bones and flesh are valuable resources in traditional Chinese medicine. In ancient times, some feudal dignitaries even regarded the Golden Monkey skin as a symbol of power and status. As a result, the hunting of Golden Monkeys never stopped. In the early 1960s, the central government listed it for first class protection; however, illegal hunting and smuggling has continued despite repeated prohibition. In recent years, the events of open hunting and killing of Golden Monkeys have gradually been reduced, but the accidental injury to the Golden Monkeys by poachers seeking to kill other animals happens occasionally and it is a threat to their survival.

For a long time, the Golden Monkey population faced the same dilemma as the giant panda. At the beginning of the 20th Century, the Golden Monkey population in the Qinling Mountains was integrated with the Sichuan population. With the increasing development of railways and roads, and the massive occupation of traditional golden monkey habitats by human reclamation and deforestation, such habitats became a number of isolated islands occupied by small groups. It is impossible for the monkeys to change their genes, so the population declined.

🐒 XI

Future
Expectations

The deteriorating condition aroused the attention of the country. Since 1998, the Chinese government began to implement a wide-ranging natural forest protection project, stopping commercial logging, and closed mountains for reforestation. In addition, the government has also implemented six major reversal projects such as transforming farmland to forests, wildlife protection, etc. The full implementation of these projects provides much better protection for Golden Monkey habitats so that the quantity of population across the country has increased substantially. Looking to the future, we believe the Golden Monkeys, a beautiful neighbor of humankind, will be better protected and developed, and the population will continue to grow.

www.ingramcontent.com/pod-product-compliance
Lightning Source LLC
Chambersburg PA
CBHW041215030426
42336CB00023B/3357

*9 7 8 0 9 9 9 7 5 1 4 0 4 *